TIME TRAVELLERS

VIKING RAIDERS

by Fiona Macdonald

Consultant: Dr. Richard Hall

ticktock
MEDIA

Copyright © ticktock Entertainment Ltd 2006
First published in Great Britain in 2005 by ticktock Media Ltd.,
Unit 2, Orchard Business Centre, North Farm Road, Tunbridge Wells, Kent TN2 3XF

ISBN 1 86007 609 2 .pbk
Printed in China

A CIP catalogue record for this book is available from the British Library.

Picture credits (t=top; b=bottom; c=centre; l=left; r=right): Alamy: 4. Graham Collins: 5tl, 12t, 14, 16l. Corbis: 6, 7tr, 7cr, 8, 9r, 10-11, 12b, 13l, 19l, 19r.
Richard Hall: 21br. Heritage Image Partnership: 17tl. PB Photo Agency: 9tl. Universitetets Oldsaksamling Oslo: 16-17. York Archaeological Trust: 13br, 15l, 21tr.
Every effort has been made to trace the copyright holders and we apologise in advance for any unintentional omissions. We would be pleased to insert the
appropriate acknowledgement in any subsequent edition of this publication.

Contents

Meet the Vikings 4

Viking adventurers 6

Ruthless raiders 8

Vikings at home 10

Viking food 12

Viking fashion 14

Deadly weapons 16

Gods and heroes 18

Living in new lands 20

The Vikings today 22

Glossary and index 24

Glossary

On page 24 there is a glossary of words and terms. The glossary words appear in **bold** in the text.

Meet the Vikings

The Vikings were bold, brave, bloodthirsty WARRIORS. They sailed from their homes in Norway, Denmark and Sweden to attack people all over Europe.

The Vikings were powerful for over 300 years, from around AD 800 to AD 1100. At first, Viking warriors were led by **warlords**. Later, they were ruled by kings.

The Vikings were not just warriors, they were also skilful sailors, busy **traders** and hard-working farmers.

4

Inside a Viking hall.

Vikings could be rough, tough and argumentative. But they also loved feasting, drinking, music, dancing, story-telling, jokes, tricks and sports!

Justice, fairness and **free speech** were very important to Viking people. They made many laws, and held the world's first **parliaments**, called *Things*.

Viking artefacts

The Vikings were brilliant boat-builders. Their **LONGSHIPS** were made from overlapping wooden planks.

Viking **CRAFT-WORKERS** carved detailed designs into wood.

This **VIKING WHISTLE** is made from a swan's leg bone. The panpipes are made from wood.

5

Viking adventurers

The Vikings loved adventure – so they sailed away on **RISKY VOYAGES**, over stormy seas. Viking explorers hoped to become famous, take over new lands and get rich!

The Vikings had no maps, but used clouds and stars to guide them. They sailed in fast warships, powered by men rowing and by the wind trapped in big, cloth sails.

A reconstruction of a Viking warship.

The Vikings sailed west and reached Iceland, Greenland and America.

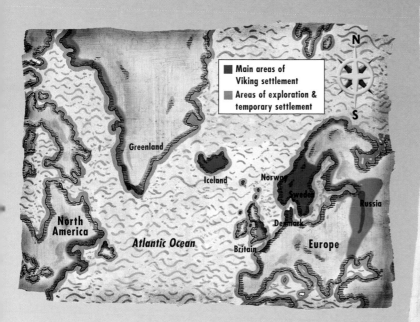

Viking **traders** travelled east through Russia. Sometimes they had to drag their ships behind them over frozen rivers. They travelled overland and along mighty rivers to reach **Middle Eastern lands**.

Viking artefacts

The Vikings fixed decorative **WEATHER VANES** on their ships' masts. They showed Viking sailors which way the wind was blowing.

Rock **ANCHORS** kept a ship in one place when it reached the shore.

This bronze Buddha statue came to Swedish Vikings from **INDIA**, after being bought and sold many times along the way.

Ruthless raiders

Viking meant **PIRATE!** The first Viking raiders sailed from their homelands to make surprise attacks on **trading centres** and **monasteries** close to the sea. Later, Viking pirates built camps in their new lands.

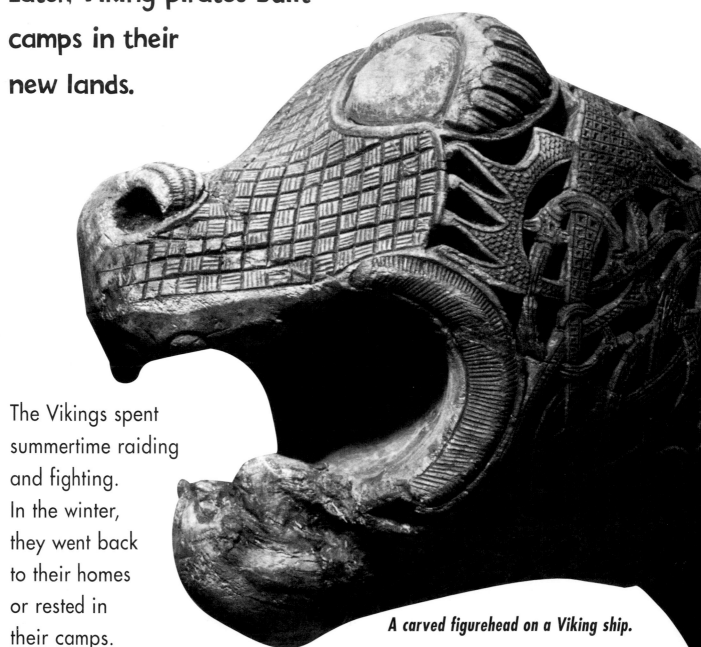

The Vikings spent summertime raiding and fighting. In the winter, they went back to their homes or rested in their camps.

A carved figurehead on a Viking ship.

Viking ships had frightening monsters on the front!

During a Viking raid, no one was safe! The Vikings attacked people in churches, monasteries, towns, villages and on farms.

Actors re-enact a Viking raid.

Viking raiders stole gold and silver and captured people to sell as **slaves**. They grabbed all they could, set fire to the rest, then hurried away.

Kings in England and France paid money to the Vikings to stop them raiding. This was called **Danegeld** (Danish money). If kings refused to pay, the Vikings killed them!

Viking artefacts

In AD 1018, Viking raiders took 37 tonnes of silver from England, as a DANEGELD PAYMENT!

CHARGE! This tombstone shows Viking raiders attacking with swords and battle-axes.

Vikings at home

Viking homes were usually made of wood. Most had just **ONE BIG ROOM**, called a hall. Outside, there were sheds for storing food and sheltering animals in wintertime.

Inside, Viking homes were smelly and stuffy. They had earth floors and some had no windows.

A reconstruction of the inside of a Viking house.

Viking homes had a smoky fire in the middle of the floor and low sleeping platforms around the walls. In the evenings, Viking families listened to stories around the fire.

History experts believe buildings like these were built for Viking royalty. They may have been used as a workshop or possibly for storage.

This is a modern-day reconstruction of a Viking building.

Actors show Viking women at work.

Viking women were in charge of the home. They cooked, cared for the children, wove cloth and made clothes.

Viking artefacts

In places like Iceland, there were no trees. So Vikings built homes of stone and **turf**. This is a modern-day turf and stone house in Iceland

Viking homes had wooden chests for storing valuables.

11

Viking food

The Vikings grew a lot of their food. Farm workers ploughed fields to grow **VEGETABLES**, such as cabbages and peas for eating in soups and stews.

Viking farmers also grew oats and barley, to make bread and beer.

This illustration shows how a Viking farm may have looked.

Viking farmers kept sheep, goats and cows. They ate their meat, made cheese from their milk and used their skins to make leather.

The Vikings also ate wild food. Using bows and arrows they hunted for deer, including reindeer, wild boar (pigs), hares, ducks, small birds and even bears.

Seabird eggs

Viking sailors caught seals, walrus and many kinds of fish to eat. Viking boys climbed cliffs to trap seabirds and collect their eggs. Girls collected seaweed, for food.

Viking artefacts

The Vikings gathered nuts, herbs, mushrooms, wild garlic and berries in meadows and forests.

Vikings drank from wooden cups or huge cows' horns.

Querns (pairs of stones that rubbed together) were used to grind oats and barley into flour.

Viking fashion

Vikings liked to **LOOK GOOD**. They chose bright colours for their clothes and trimmed them with fur, braid and embroidery. Both men and women styled their hair and wore homemade make-up.

Viking men wore tunics and trousers, and women wore long dresses, pinafores and shawls. To keep warm, everyone wore hats, boots and cloaks.

Beautiful brooches, made of gold, silver or cheaper metals, were used to fasten clothes. Vikings also wore bead necklaces, bracelets and rings.

Viking neckrings and beads.

The Vikings kept clean in saunas. They heated rocks in a fire, then poured on water to create clouds of steam. They sat in the steam and sweated to clean away the dirt.

Viking artefacts

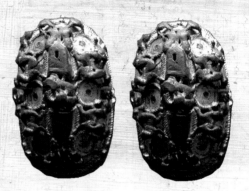

Viking women wore pairs of oval brooches, one on each shoulder.

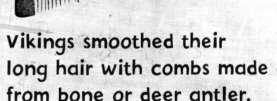

Vikings smoothed their long hair with combs made from bone or deer antler.

Warriors were given armbands as rewards for **FIGHTING BRAVELY**. They wore them with pride!

Deadly weapons

Vikings valued **COURAGE** more than life itself! Viking warriors joined armies led by kings and **warlords**, and swore to follow them loyally. Warriors hoped to win glory by fighting bravely, and to be remembered long after they had died.

Viking warriors fought with bows and arrows, battle-axes, spears and swords. They wore tunics of padded leather and protected their bodies with wooden shields. Some Viking chiefs and top warriors wore **chain mail** armour.

A Berserker warrior chess piece.

Berserker (bear-shirt) warriors worked themselves up into a fury before a battle. They put on bear-skin cloaks, ground their teeth, chewed their shields, then fought furiously!

Vikings wore metal helmets to protect their heads. The helmets had protective strips around the eyes and a nose-guard.

Viking warriors gave their favourite swords vicious names, such as SHARP BITER or VIPER (KILLER SNAKE).

An axe head from a Viking battle-axe. They were used to HACK ENEMIES TO DEATH.

Spears were for throwing long distances, when ENEMIES tried to escape.

Gods and heroes

The Vikings believed that gods **RULED THE WORLD**. Vikings **sacrificed** dogs, horses and even people to please their gods.

Thor, was the lord of thunderstorms. Vikings said he made lightning flash across the sky. Thor was very big and very strong – but rather stupid!

A Valkyrie

A bronze statue of Thor.

Vikings believed that *Valkyries* (warrior goddesses) carried the souls of dead **heroes** to *Valhalla* – a great Viking hall in the sky. There, the heroes fought all day and feasted all night.

Odin was the greatest Viking god of all. Brave and clever, he brought victory in battle.

This Viking picture stone shows Odin riding his magic horse.

Odin rode a magic, eight-legged horse across the sky. Two ravens (birds that ate the flesh of dead warriors) flew beside him. The ravens' names were Thought and Memory.

Viking artefacts

For **GOOD LUCK**, vikings wore lucky charms shaped like Thor's mighty hammer.

This Viking **TOMBSTONE** is carved with spiky letters called **runes**. The Vikings believed that runes had magic powers.

19

Living in new lands

Over the years, many Vikings left their homes, and looked for **NEW PLACES** to live. Some vikings wanted to find better farmland. Others wanted to run their own lives, away from new, powerful Viking kings.

The Vikings settled in Scotland, England, Ireland, France, Iceland and Greenland.

Other Vikings, called *Rus*, settled in eastern Europe. The land where they lived is still known as Russia today.

A Viking called Leif *(the Lucky)* Eriksson was the first **European** to land in North America, around AD 1000.

A modern-day statue of Leif Eriksson.

Some Vikings settled in North America, but they quarrelled among themselves and fought with the Native Americans. They left after just a few years.

Viking settlements

A Viking settlement was found in York in England. This picture shows **archaeolog**ists digging up Viking remains.

This is a modern reconstruction of one of the buildings from the Viking settlement in North America.

The Vikings today

Many Viking words are still used today in lands where the Vikings once settled. In English, Viking words include sky, knife, ship, bang, birth, deaf, fang, freckle and egg.

Many Viking burials have survived. When excavated (dug up), they tell us about life in Viking times.

This is the Oseberg Viking ship.

This ship was found under a large mound in a field at Oseberg in Norway. A Viking queen and her servant girl were buried inside.

Some Viking activities such as ski-ing and skating are still very popular today. Viking hunters used skis to chase animals across snowy ground.

A Viking ice skate

The Vikings went ice-skating on frozen lakes with skates made from animal bones.

Viking artefacts

← **Birsay A 967**

Many places still have Viking names. Birsay, on the Orkney Islands, means HUNTING GROUND ISLAND in the Viking language.

Some days of the week are still called after Viking gods. Thursday is named for THOR and Friday for FREYJA, the goddess of love. This Viking pendant shows Freyja.

23

Glossary

ARCHAEOLOGISTS People who dig things up to study history.

BERSERKER A Viking warrior. Berserkers wore bear-skin cloaks. They worked themselves up into a fury before a battle to be extra fierce!

CHAIN MAIL Amour made of thousands of small metal rings linked together.

DANEGELD Payments made to the Vikings by French and English kings, to stop them raiding.

EUROPEAN A person from one of the countries of Europe.

FREE SPEECH Freedom to talk about ideas, beliefs and opinions, without fear of punishment or discrimination.

HEROES Men and women who are exceptionally brave, strong, daring or good.

MIDDLE EASTERN LANDS Countries that are today known as Syria, Lebanon, Jordan, Israel and Palestine.

MONASTERIES Communities of monks – men who have devoted their lives to God. They live, work and pray together.

PARLIAMENTS Meetings to discuss the best way of running a country or a community. Parliaments make laws, set punishments and make important decisions about community life.

RECONSTRUCTION Something that is made in modern times to look like something from history. For example, a building.

RUNES The writing of the Vikings.

SACRIFICED Killed as an offering to gods and goddesses.

SLAVES People who belonged to someone else. They had to work for their owners and could be bought or sold.

TRADERS People who make a living from buying and selling.

TRADING CENTRES Places where farmers, craftworkers and travelling merchants met to buy and sell.

TURF Slabs of earth and grass.

WARLORDS Powerful men who were good at fighting. They had their own private armies of loyal warriors who fought for them.

Index

C
crafts — 5

D
Danegeld — 9

E
explorers — 6, 7

F
farming — 12, 13
fashion — 14, 15
food — 12, 13

G
gods — 18, 19, 23

H
heroes — 18
homes — 10, 11, 21

J
jewellery — 15

N
names (Viking) — 23

O
Odin — 19

R
raids — 8, 9
runes — 19

S
settlements — 20, 21

T
Thor — 18
traders — 4, 7

V
Viking life — 5

W
warriors — 4, 16
weapons — 16, 17
women — 11
words (Viking) — 22